THE
ROYAL
MILE

Text © Jim Crumley, 1989
Photographs © Marius Alexander, 1989
Drawings © Richard Demarco, 1989

Published by Moubray House Publishing Limited,
Tweeddale Court, 14 High Street,
The Royal Mile,
Edinburgh EH1 1TE

Designed by Dorothy Steedman
Typeset in-house in Garamond ITC
by Moubray House Publishing Ltd.
Colour separations, printing and binding
by Imago Publishing Ltd.
Printed in Italy

ISBN 0 948473 14 2

THE
ROYAL
MILE

From Palace To Castle
Scotland's Most Romantic Way

Text Jim Crumley
Photographs Marius Alexander
Drawings Richard Demarco

MOUBRAY HOUSE PUBLISHING
THE ROYAL MILE, EDINBURGH

HIGH STREET, LAWNMARKET & CASTLEHILL   Richard Demarco

 The strong historical link between Scotland and Scandinavia influenced the decision of the fastest growing Scandinavian hotel chain to choose Edinburgh for its latest hotel. The design of the Scandic Crown Hotel in Edinburgh's Royal Mile is influenced by traditional Scottish architecture and its situation offers residents an opportunity to enjoy one of Scotland's most romantic and historic settings.

 The Burrell Company is a Scottish property group based in Edinburgh whose speciality is residential development. Old Assembly Close, a major restoration of a 19th century building in the Royal Mile, is one of the Burrell Company's many current developments which emphasise the importance of good design in blending the old with the new.

Published with the support of the Scandic Crown Hotel and the Burrell Company.

Nature is chief architect in the Old Town of Edinburgh. A volcanic plug and its glacial tail dwindling down to the east offered a defendable plinth for those first shadowy settlers who trod the wake of the retreating ice. An abrupt cliff rendered the west not negotiable; and a loch and a quagmire discouraged settlement or invasion of the valley to the north; a deeper, sheerer valley excluded the south. So those settlers, their thatchers and carpenters, stonemasons and architects, who have layered the place with all their civilisations since the ice, have simply aped nature's actions, setting stone on stone, cliff on cliff, spine on spine, crown on crown. For all that we have since bridged canyons, drained and tamed wild loch and bog, sprawled the crown, smoothed the cliffs and soothed the spine, the principles of even today's Old Town remain the legacy of that glacial upheaval.

It would begin with a speculative scanning of the ridge from the sea. It would seem a sound place. Wise heads in the bows would confer, their wisdoms honed by daring, thwarting outwitting, surviving. A party might land, tread the hill warily for fear of foe or beast, climbing from its lowest seaward ebb to its blunt rock crown, marvelling at expanding horizons. Birch and whin and oak and pine would fankle their progress, petering out as the uncompromising summit rock petered in. They would agree that this was a sound place to fortify.

Whatever may have changed since then and whenever 'then' may have been, there can be few more enduring and unbroken lineages in the history of our built environment than the route we have become accustomed to call the Royal Mile, the single street from the Palace of Holyroodhouse to the Castle which is at once the spine and the heart and the womb of Edinburgh's Old Town.

It would begin with a speculative scanning of the ridge from the sea . . .

In its gray midst, the Royal Mile remains brave and impressive.
There are few places in the land where the sense of stepping in history's sod is quite so tangible, and none - other than, say, the Pass of Glencoe on a morbid day of November rains and truculent snows - which so harbours and holds its aura of destiny. For this single street has been a stupendous stage for many of Scotland's dramas, and almost all the stars of her history.

That aura is an omnipresence, veined with sleights of hand and subtleties of mood and character which dilute and intensify it by turns, sometimes with a charismatic flair quite unsuspected in the repertoire of a city often misrepresented as the dour hub of John Knox's little empire; sometimes with the clammy cape of a sodden easterly haar about its shoulders, which can stifle sights and sounds and any sense of the world beyond for half a week.

Whatever the magics and malevolences of such moods, however, they rely for their effect on the stage they play. It is first a crammed place, heaped with built stone, a tumbling riverbed of gray setts from which the stone-flagged tributaries of the closes spill and slither. The closes, instinctive rhythmic solution of centuries of stonemasons, also bring a semblance of ragged order to nature's chaos. They tunnel deepest into the weave of the Old Town fabric, offer furtive glimpses of its old stone soul, and still have the capacity to surprise leisured strollers and astound hardened historians not easy to impress, by revealing fragments of their barely believable oldness. It is a phenomenon of this simplicity of design - the tributaries flowing north and south from a parent river flowing west to east - that the juxtaposition of the two can create adjacent and opposite miniature climates of light and shade, storm and sanctuary.

For the second characteristic of the Royal Mile as a stage is that it is a high and windy place, so that the light and the air are seldom still. The closes offer not just tunnels but funnels, not just windtraps but windbreaks, not just stone burrows but sunshafts and shadowshafts, counteractions and contradictions. They weave a rich tapestry. They also offer fleeting immunity from the sea fog. Of all the moods of the place, it is that phenomenon - the haar - which most displeases its weather-weary citizenry: a miles-wide cocoon of restless, airy ooze which obliterates

The Castle from Salisbury Crags: *They would agree that this was a sound place to fortify*

8

the Castle from its rock and severs the Tron Kirk steeple at its clockface; which rolls among the corbels and the crowsteps and shines the setts; which stalks the streets with all the energy of a puffball in a windless desert; which seeps gray ice into a human heart.

Yet step out into a Royal Mile swaddled in such a wet blanket - particularly at night when the street lights make a sodden bonfire of the air - and this most lived-in of city centres reduces its population to a huddle of hearths. The susceptible mind's eye can banish centuries in circumstances like these, when nature's architectural influences reassert themselves to unshackle the place from its perspectives and period pieces. The Royal Mile becomes again the whole city and nothing but the city, and you begin to grasp the significance of where you are, in the old stone heart of a city which invented its New Town more than 200 years ago, by which time its Old Town was already decrepit, scavenged by kites, and as raucous and reeking as a Bass Rock gannetry in June.

In the haar of a March night then, pause by Knox's House and dare the preacher himself to hurry in upstairs, throwing a black look and a mediaeval profanity over his shoulder at the weather. Fill your ears with the clatterings of horse and cartwheel and cobble and street trader, and the sudden military flourish scattering them all as a Stuart Queen rides home late. Fill your mind's eye with the Jacobite Prince courting disaster amid the claret-fuelled cheer of Holyrood; thread the closes with the furtive bodysnatching darts of Burke and Hare; populate the pubs with Coven-anters and Whigs and Jacobites and poets and painters and every manner of walking street life down to a stray dog and a rat. This street has known and shrugged off them all.

There are three seasons in the Royal Mile, or rather two and two halves. Spring and autumn are seasons which happen to other people. There are few enough gardens or trees worth the name to remark on bud or blossom or leaf-fall. Old Royal Mile hands record the advent of other people's springs by a softening and slowing of the wind, other people's autumns by the 'sale' signs in the souvenir shops and the slow creep of the shadow of St Giles up the north wall of the street.

Either side of the long showpiece summer there is a languid no-man's-land-of-the-seasons which buffers it from winter. Of course, nothing

It is a high and windy place, so that the light and the air are seldom still

11

in the Old Town is as definable as all that. There are days when the seasons trip over each other four at a time, and years when winter never gives up its wearying ghost. Although, when the city's arena of hills whitens and the sandstone sparkles, and the natives can call the place their own, winter can be the stateliest of all Edinburgh's garbs. It is a sharp, acquired taste, like an Islay malt, but once you cultivate a drouth for the winter city you have won the perception of the connoisseur.

Summer puts colour back into the Royal Mile's cheeks, dresses the wan sandstone in flags and Festival finery, gives the stage a strut and a kilted swagger of its own. The street thrums heady with coaches and a perambulating Babel of voices. Then the Royal Mile is an endless trek of discovery. Every day of every summer, thousands discover for themselves what thousands more discovered the day before, and thousands more will discover the day after. The cheek-by-jowl nature of the street as a living community simply adds to the fascination of the visitor (and whiles, the mild frustration of the natives). But in a sense, that was always the Royal Mile's lot. Today's summer invasion is just one more era laying its own small claim to a phenomenal posterity.

The world has always beaten a path to this door. Whatever the motives of the travellers, they have found things to marvel at here and, in the tradition of the first settlers from the sea, and all the great processions ever since, the trek begins at the foot of 'the Mile', because the architecture of Nature demands it.

THE ROYAL MILE FROM CALTON HILL

Richard Demarco

DAVID AND THE STAG

In the beginning
a fortress drawbridged
down an unroyal mile
of rock. All Edinburgh

spilled from that womb
umbilically led
by the vision
of a hunting king.

Providence - or whatever -
deflected the stag's
goring advance on
death's door's king

whose eternal gratitude
built an abbey
which built a palace
which built the Canongate

which makes at least
half-a-mile royal. Now
the Canongate commemorates
only the stag.

*The Palace of
Holyroodhouse and its
Abbey have not lost
their power to impress*

In the twilight today we went to the Palace where Queen Mary lived and loved . . . the chapel beside it has now lost its roof, it is overgrown with grass and ivy, and at the broken altar, Mary was crowned Queen of Scotland. Everything is ruined, decayed and open to the sky. I believe I have found there today the beginning of my Scotch Symphony . . .

The Palace of Holyroodhouse and its Abbey have not lost their power to impress and compel since Felix Mendelssohn found a sanctuary for his muse there in 1829. Today's pilgrim may have nothing more profound in mind than a gentle brush with the artefacts of Scotland's destiny. But if you will pursue its spoor up that single grimed and gloried hill we call the Royal Mile, you will find that Holyrood still harbours the beginning of a symphony of stone. You will also find that Holyrood remains Mary's. For all the heroes and villains who followed her, for all the kings and would-be kings and conquerors, for all their masons and architects and artists who nurtured their whims, and all the chroniclers and bards who immortalised their claims to fame and infamy, the spirit of Mary, Queen of Scots, has never relinquished its exquisitely sorrowing pervasiveness.

She dug-in the heels of Catholicism in the Edinburgh of Knox's outraged mob; she threw her flame-haired glances on the crass and fushionless Darnley when she might have won the heart of any lord in the land. She turned to the sly, flattering intellect of Riccio and the concerted jealousies of her Court, fearing a Papist mole, put a brutal and bloody end to his glamorous (and probably purely platonic) association with the Queen.

Knox, practising rare discretion, slunk off to Ayr, finding the whole wretched episode thoroughly just, doubtless giving his dour God the credit, and entreating Him to destroy 'the whore in her whoredom'. Although, if Antonia Fraser's biography of Mary might be judged a less partial assessment than Knox's, she was the first and last frigid whore in and out of Christendom.

Mary's apartments remain an aloof sanctuary for the spirit of her life and times. They are unregally cramped and eerily cloaked in an intangible presence which neither the gaudy painted ceilings of her day nor the prosaic delivery of the Palace guide can dispel. Mary's spirit is the truest

Holyrood Abbey: *'Everything is ruined, decayed and open to the sky.'*

relic of untainted Scottishness in the building which confronts today's visitor, that north-west tower where she lived the truest architectural expression of her spirit. That expression, which is echoed uniquely across the Scottish landscape in scores of free-standing tower houses, has been subdued at Holyrood. Mary's apartments are ill-at-ease in the concocted late-seventeenth century grandeur of the Palace and its Victorian and twentieth century embellishments and afterthoughts. It seems churlish to quarrel with an architectural legacy 300 years after the event, especially one as gracious and fabled and glamorous as Holyrood Palace. In a sense, though, there is a clue here to what you will find as you thread the patched and darned - and whiles threadbare - stone fabric of the Royal Mile. The seventeenth century palace took Mary's tower as its first point of reference, matching its well-weathered bulk with a replica facade at the south-west corner, but grafting between and behind an arcaded quadrangle of a scale and elegance quite unenvisaged by James V's stonemasons when they set out to do their master's bidding and built the tower. The result is spectacular, distinguished, regal, fitted to grander notions of monarchies, but not instinctively indigenous, at odds with the Old Town as James V's tower never was. Holyrood remains true to its origins only once you have crossed Mary's threshhold.

The Royal Mile sometimes forgets itself, too, with flights of inappropriate fancy. Some of them are much too recent for our comfort, but it has won its centuries of distinction - and continues to win them even now - by falling back almost exclusively on its mediaeval origins. It masks the infinite variations of its centuries behind closed ranks of many-storeyed stone and harling, adhering to the main theme of the symphony. The result is only rarely spectacular (at those few memorable points along its length where it offers sudden far-flung perspectives from its gently weaving canyon), frequently inelegant, but it distinguishes itself as a worthy and, crucially, a living epitaph to its first instinctive stonemasons, and to nature's rock.

So the Palace impresses most as it ages, a fact acknowledged by today's guides who leave Mary until last, usher you from her apartments and leave you to your own devices in the Abbey. This sudden unshackling (after the crowding and shepherding and tapsalteerie deluge of facts and

Mary's apartments remain an aloof sanctuary for the spirit of her life and times

dates and portraits and ceilings and walk-this-way-don't-touch and wasn't-Bonnie-Prince-Charlie-blond?) has an uninhibiting effect utterly appropriate to the Abbey's stupendous skeleton. Here, at last, you can go your own way and look and touch and feel the coarse craft six centuries old, and marvel at the stonemason's pinnacled art, where the packed stone walls simply curve up and on to form a roof of crude and breathtaking grace.

There is, too, shuttered from public gaze, and preserved now for no reason than its own fragmentary self, a small piece of the very first abbey, a sliver of the twelfth century, a tattered period piece which startles simply with its age and its hodden workmanship. Here is a familiar theme in the Royal Mile, a percussive recurring undercurrent to the symphony; a building establishes its own mood and antiquity and is cherished and valued accordingly (the cherishing by degrees, related to the benevolence of its mood; the valuing, to its impact on the townscape) until there is sudden cause to pare away a layer of some century-or-other's veneer, and an old, old throwback stands revealed in all its musty majesty.

Holyrood Abbey's oldest throwback is more than that, however. It is the one tangible evidence which links this dwindling twentieth century with the best, the most durable legend in the Royal Mile. The date of whatever happened is agreed at least - September 14, 1128. That, and that there was an extraordinary event, which so troubled King David that he felt compelled - or was prevailed upon - to build an abbey 'in the little valley between two mountains' by way of gratitude.

It was Rood-day ('Rood' is simply the cross) and the Feast of the Exaltation of the Cross. The King's confessor counselled a day of devotion; the King, unpersuaded, went hunting in the forest of Drumsheugh instead. (It is a phenomenon to contemplate; that great swathe of Lothian forest niggling at the feet of the embryonic rock-clinging city and its loch, and dominated by Calton Hill and Arthur's Seat and the Pentland prow, a wilderness scene now barely credible.) David became separated from his party, whether by accident, design, or divine intervention, and was suddenly trapped by crag and thick forest into a confrontation with a stag at bay. The stag, already infuriated by

. . . . the concocted late seventeenth century grandeur of the Palace and its Victorian and twentieth century embellishments and afterthoughts

23

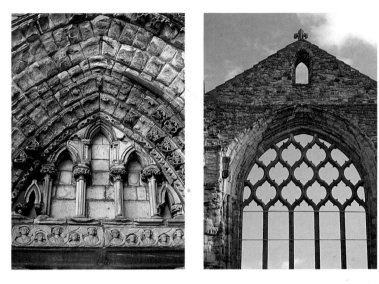

. . . the Abbey's stupendous skeleton. Here at last you can go your own way and look and touch and feel the coarse craft six centuries old

the beaters (and possibly stirred into some agitation by the impending onset of the rut if it was a red deer), turned on the King. David fell from his horse, futilely armed with only a short sword. With the destiny of Scotland at the stag's mercy, a silver cloud suddenly bore a cross between the beast's antlers, offering the King an unlikely straw to clutch and the stag a cue to flee.

Some variations of the aftermath embroider David's subsequent pondering with a vision of St Andrew; another variation of the entire episode attributes the crucifix's intervention to the powers of the Black Rood which David inherited from his mother and always wore, and which he would have invoked in that dark hour.

The legend endures, commemorated in the badge of the Canongate, and the abbey he built spawned an abbot's house which spawned a royal tower house which spawned a palace. History has never tired here. Symphonies will stir and kindle in lesser men than Mendelssohn.

Holyrood and the remnants and restorations of Abbey Strand which flank the modern Palace entrance, stand apart from the climbing curve of the Royal Mile beyond, severed by the demands of late twentieth century traffic management. It is an illusory aloofness, however, for in the Abbey's heyday it offered doorstep sanctuary for the teeming commoners beyond. A last refuge of debtors from their pursuers, of criminals from what passed for justice, in eras when the theft of a loaf or the failure to notify a pregnancy were hanging offences.

Cross the brass plates set in the street at the mouth of the Abbey Strand and you cross the frontier of sanctuary, there to take your chances in the bowels of the city, the high-walled canyon of the Canongate. Here the fact and artefact of history crowd in, lurk under every other lintel and peer out from every other closemouth; a place to ambush your senses. This is the bottom of the world, the rest of which lies unguessed at, beyond the first discreet meandering curve of the old stone riverbed. Edinburgh is another world. The Canongate was its own strong-willed burgh, half-a-Royal Mile, uphill.

First steps in the Canongate introduce two of its twentieth century heroes in Patrick Geddes and Robert Hurd. Geddes won the epitaph of 'the father of town planning' by his timely recognition (at the turn of this century) of the worth of his surroundings, of how much of the mediaeval city was lost, how much still survived and how much of that was at risk. Hurd was an architect who practised the conviction he preached: that the Scottish architectural tradition was a force with a future as well as an immortal past; that people, particularly Scots, responded to it uniquely with an instinctive warmth. He brought his philosophy to bear on telling restorations and crucial patchwork darning in the fabric of the Royal Mile. He gave the symphony back some of its best songs.

The twin visions of Geddes and Hurd coincided in the Canongate and established precedents for even humble tenements: that seventeenth and eighteenth century restorations were more appropriate than any-thing the twentieth century might divine. Much had already been lost, but much of the rot - which had diseased attitudes as well as buildings - was stopped by their efforts. New attitudes towards Edinburgh's oldest built heritage were forged on the anvil of their creativity.

The Canongate is rich in vigour, in its sense of community which not even the clearances of the 1960s to nearby Dumbiedykes and distant suburbs has been quite able to annihilate. At first glance it seems a gray place, conspicuously free from child-chant and street life, abandoned to tourism at the expense of families, a repository for the past, but it simply lives quietly, and colour, once you know where to look, is everywhere. It is firstly - and least obviously - in its people. For although the pavements thicken from time to time with the strolling world taking its tourist's ease, and although the best of the Canongate's restorations and re-buildings are priced well beyond the grasp of many of those hapless displaced burghers of the 1960s, there is still a quiet thrumming of old Edinburgh's heart here which is the vital pulse of its own people.

They are a discreet tribe, these descendants of the mediaeval mob which once ruled the streets - this of all streets - with a swift and often violent flourish of its own definition of justice; they grow conspicuous and voluble only when you pare away the layers of tourism's cosmetic, or catch the old burgh unawares in its sharp out-of-season garb. A stairhead or a shopfront greeting is a clue (visitors do neither) to a Canogotian encounter. Or, penetrate the murk of the Tolbooth Tavern where beer and bacardi flow over the precise spot where their forebears once slumped wordlessly, lifelessly down from the trapdoor beneath the hangman's noose.

This discretion is a mask of a unique evolution, and it is often mistaken by outsiders and incomers for the stamp of a race apart, apathetic, aloof. It is none of these things. For the asking, here is as much ready warmth and humour, and wit and wisdom, and human failings and follies, as in any half mile in the land. For the asking.

But the native of a place like the Canongate has his character shaped and whittled by the accumulated burdens of rubbing shoulders with greatness for a living, of nudging immortality as a fact of everyday life. So many greatnesses have gathered here over so many centuries; so many millions of the admirers and disciples of greatnesses traipse their pilgrimages here. So much that they hold unique is common-or-garden here so that the native harbours his own awareness close and confronts the wondering world beyond his lintel with a philosophical shrug. It is a protective shrug, but cut him and he bleeds pride and a sense of place in time's atlas. He knows his worth in the continuity of the story of his street, knows that if his tribe should ever wither, the last spark of the Canongate's old old soul would be snuffed. He would have you believe it was snuffed long since, in the heights of the Royal Mile beyond. So the colour of the natives may be cloaked in the hodden gray of a humdrum shrug, but its true unshrugged shades are as rich as any Stuart queen's ceilings.

Colour glitters too from the buildings. The older the brighter. White Horse Close is a fragment of Holland washed up in that old tide of trade which ebbed and flowed across the North Sea, which marked its passage in much of Scottish painting and the architecture of the east coast, especially the Forth shores of Fife and East Lothian. The close is cool and quiet, colour rich in its cascades of pots. It is a reverential 1962 restoration of the White Horse Inn of 1623. Almost too reverential, you

White Horse Close

fear, for contemporary illustrations invariably show the inn awash with the bustle and bedlam of a place which worked for its living. Now the signs proclaim 'No Ball Games' - a familiar song in the Royal Mile courts and closes - a greeting which always makes me want to put another sign beside it saying 'Why?' What was the pivotal point in the Royal Mile's history which turned away children and their games? What is wrong with children? Why are there almost none, and how is the street to perpetuate its unquestionable destiny without them?

It is easy to step into White Horse Close and fall in love with it and fall to pondering the conundrum that this very restoration was being plotted at the same time as a substantial proportion of the Canongate's native population was being soullessly relegated to the fringes of the city. Small wonder, then, that its charm finds more favour with visitors and 'all-our-yesterdays' film producers than with cynics and Canongate survivors.

This colour-questing finds more riches in even the unsunny cloister of Bakehouse Close. The arched pend may seem a blackened and forbidding deterrent, but with its furtive glimpse into the old stone treas-ure store of Huntly House (the vast, stunning mansion-turned-museum which straddles the close) and the arching wizardry of its roof, it is a sesame to perhaps the best close in town. The sun does penetrate fleetingly here, and what it does for the rubble masonry above the back of the pend is to pinpoint purples and pinks, golds, reds and tawnies in that wall you once called gray. A white-harled crowstep gable, so worn and centuries-weary that it has barely a right-angle left in its frayed geometry, climbs above you with all the dizzy vigour of Sgurr Alasdair's Pinnacle Ridge in the Skye Cuillins. It is the privilege of beautifully crafted and well-worn built stone to evoke such a justifiable analogy with the best of natural sculpture. Bakehouse Close gets closer to the essence of the Royal Mile than most other places, because it largely locks out the present, because it demonstrates the art of the close as a second street of its own.

Its neighbour, Acheson House, is one of many mansions which flourished in the Canongate, and although it is now the Scottish Craft Centre (none of the Canongate's mansions are still lived in as private homes) and normally entered by the side door from the Royal Mile, its

the braggart gusto of Huntly House

31

small forecourt, off the close, reveals a majestically proportioned yet somehow humble frontage. It is Scottish architecture at its most instinctively satisfying, a building with a sense of place. Here is none of the braggart gusto of Huntly House and its vast (for the Royal Mile) street frontage and moralising wall-mounted mottoes carved in stone; only an unwritten eloquence on its walls, a simplistic sense of style. It was built in 1633 and restored by Robert Hurd for the Marquess of Bute in 1937. It should be lived in by people, but the Scottish Craft Centre, one of the twentieth century's worthier innovations in the Canongate, is a fit occupancy.

For all the Royal Mile's dalliances with the Lord and his infinite manifestations in built stone, the Canongate's is the only kirkyard to survive. I subscribe to James Grant's assessment of the Canongate Kirk in his *Old and New Edinburgh*: 'a most unpicturesque-looking edifice of nameless style, with a species of Doric porch'. For all that, and the dull cross-shaped bulk which that edifice never quite masks, the place commands attention, even affection, and has gathered about its seventeenth century skirts quite a kirkyard congregation of celebrated souls.

Chief among them was surely George Drummond, six times Lord Provost of Edinburgh between 1725 and 1760. His claims to fame are astonishing for one man in one city. He was the champion of the University and the instigator of the Royal Infirmary, friend of Hanoverian Kings and foe of the Jacobite cause, to the extent of mustering a farcical and quite abortive defence of the city against Bonnie Prince Charlie in 1745, and volunteering to join Cope at Dunbar. He chose his civic campaigns with rather more distinction than his military ones. He is remembered still as the Father of the New Town for daring to dream of a new, purpose-built, elegant Edinburgh beyond the squalid and swarming confines of the old Rock, beyond the Nor' Loch. Although he died before the New Town was born, he effected the quantum leap of thought which flung the North Bridge out from the heart of the Royal Mile and over the Nor' Loch's valley. That single stroke of genius unlocked the whole New Town enterprise and his spirit is still invoked to spur those hours when Edinburgh drags its heels in civic endeavour. Drummond's Canongate Kirkyard memorial is a curiously discreet stone for one so honoured in his own lifetime - and

Canongate Kirk: *commands attention, even affection, and has gathered about its seventeenth century skirts quite a kirkyard congregation of celebrated souls*

Butts Close   Richard Demarco

ever since - but a Royal Mile pilgrimage will eventually encounter his ultimate Old Town memorial, high above the Canongate, near the summit of the High Street.

No such graveyard discretion marks the last resting place of Adam Smith, the crackpot intellectual who wrote *The Wealth of Nations* and *The Theory of Moral Sentiments*, two milestones of Scottish academic achievement. (Smith lived from 1778 until his death in 1790 in nearby Panmure House, another calmly articulate seventeenth century mansion of great charm.) He is commemorated flamboyantly on the hideous back wall of one of those bizarre stone 'bathing huts' which characterises Edinburgh kirkyards of antiquity; catch the place in the wrong frame of mind or with the haar moistening the bony brow of the Kirk's stag-head crown, and who knows what manner of hellish legions of bathers might sally out to trouble a fearful mind's eye? Someone thought to floor Smith's cubicle in pink chips, a goonish splash of colour amid the kirkyard's all-pervasive green and gray.

Not all the Canongate's deserving dead achieved cubicle status. A near neighbour of Adam Smith was plucked by Robert Burns from a pauper's grave and set here in a truer perspective. These words appear on the headstone at Burns' insistence:

Here lies Robert Fergusson, poet.
Born September 5, 1751, died October 16, 1774.

No sculptured Marble here nor pompous lay
No storied Urn nor animated Bust
This simple Stone directs Pale Scotia's way
To pour her Sorrows o'er her Poet's Dust.

Alas, Pale Scotia has saved her sorrowing for other causes. Fergusson is as unsung and unlamented as he is uncelebrated. He has this stone, that bench by the Kirk wall, and two centuries of oblivion to mark his young heyday here. His street-wise poetry, especially of the stinking, stupendous Old Town he was born into, and the brief and viciously uprooted flowering of his muse, are less than hero-worshipped. He was the root from which Burns blossomed on Edinburgh's stage. Burns was as generous

Richard Demarco at
work: the Demarco
Gallery has been based
in the Old Town for
many years

THE BAGMAN

He treads
his ground-down groove
through streets
so stone-by-stone familiar
he forgets
what they look like.

Stoop-by-stoop
a slow avalanche of coats
burdens shoulders bowed
by the demands
of a studious addiction
to the perpetual pavement's
next gray yard.

He pounds
history's beat obliviously
(the feted Prince
the fated Marquess . . .
such are the feet
which signed this street)
a day-by-day destiny
with victories commemorated
in hot meals, defeats
in cold, cold nights.

One day in spring he lifts
his sun-slit eyes a while
to throw a pretty face
a royal smile.

as Edinburgh and Scotland have been ungenerous since. Burns from far Alloway, won for his Edinburgh memorial a temple on Calton Hill, a window in St Giles, and a worldwide ritualistic supper which strays ever further from the truth, while Fergusson, the Royal Mile's own poet languishes unsung. We will weave Fergusson's song again into this symphony, for the Royal Mile should do him prouder than this.

Across the kirkyard there is one more simple stone to acknowledge. It says this, to which nothing need be added: *Robert Hurd, architect, 1905-1963, whose works included much restoration and new building in the Canongate.*

There is, finally, a tall memorial in the furthest flung corner of the kirkyard, to the soldiers who died between 1692 and 1880: *In Edinburgh Castle situated in the Parish of Canongate.* That is how it once was hereabouts. That is the old significance of where you stand.

Where you stand, there he sits, near the Mercat Cross in a corner of the kirkyard. They are ancient survivors both, he and the cross, and the one about as hard to date as the other. He is a Bagman, a wanderer, a tramp, a down and out, a bum, call him what you will. The sun-facing benches of the Canongate kirkyard are as fixed an abode as he has. His world is two, three, whiles four coats, depending on the season and his luck. The cap is ever present, but in winter one more coat is often gathered over that and his shoulders, so that to chance on his shuffled progress up the Mile from behind and in the dark is to confront a black, headless apparition. He appears to have a territory bounded on the south by the north side of the Royal Mile, on the north by Waverley Station, on the west by a quiet bench in Princes Street Gardens, on the east by the bench in the Kirkyard.

This he patrols more or less wordlessly, like a roding woodcock, occasionally raising his eye to you two or three seasons of the year, but not, as far as I know, in winter. Winter, keep the head down, coat-capped. It is all done with a single speed, a good grace, and as little movement as possible. If you can sit the day out warm and untroubled, sit it out. His capacity for thought, or thoughtlessness is vast and enviable.

I encountered him once on a black Christmas Eve, too cold for sitting. I was driving, crushed between a taxi and an impatient bus. He was

The Tolbooth:
*venerable old hub of
the Canongate,
excruciatingly
disfigured by a
Victorian clock*

BAKEHOUSE CLOSE

Richard Demarco

The Canongate
brightens as it climbs

FORSYTH OF EDINBURGH.

At first glance, it seems a gray place, but colour, once you know where to look for it, is everywhere

standing near the top of the Canongate. He had been walking uphill, and ran out of fuel, and because it was too cold for sitting, he simply stopped and stood. Pedestrians treated him like a roundabout. The bus hooted unfestive irritation. I moved off, caught a final dark glimpse of him in my mirror. I wished him peace on his earth, goodwill to all Bagmen.

I invest him with reincarnations. Darnley? No, not dreary enough. Fergusson? No, not young enough. Drummond? No, he was thirled in his later years to the fields beyond the Nor' Loch. Smith? Aye, mebbe. Brilliant, but fey. A dishevelled, perpetual thinker. The wealth of his nations in two carrier bags.

The Canongate brightens as it climbs. Colour washed walls infiltrate the stone ramparts. Your uphill glance from the Tolbooth anticipates them with relish, but the venerable old hub of the Canongate stops your tracks like a Bagman out of fuel. This was the council chamber and much else besides, built in 1593, and excruciatingly disfigured by a Victorian clock whose stag's head owes more to Glenfiddich than David I. Its new role is as a People's Story museum, an oral history archive of the Canongate's living memory. Eventually, that municipal brainwave may well demonstrate more tellingly than we can imagine, just how much has gone.

On a late-March late-afternoon with the last of the light in the west sky and the first of the house lights on, I followed the Bagman's groove up the Canongate, and threw an idle glance up at Moray House's arrogant jutting balcony, a place designed not so much for seeing from, but to be seen on. There was a light in an upstairs room, which because of all the street's gathered shadows, threw its renaissance plaster ceilings into vivid focus. Every detail was so clear from the street and the whole building so free from every other detail of the civilising influences of the intervening centuries (this is the occasional time-warping privilege of an all-season familiarity with this street), that I threw my mind energetically into rebuilding one of the Royal Mile's most infamous processions.

That lighted room spilled guests in heady, party mood onto the balcony. There was much to celebrate for the Covenanting Argyll and his tribe. They were in the throes of his son's wedding party, and the

doomed James Graham, Marquess of Montrose was to be led beneath that balcony on his last journey, betrayed by the same Argyll, to be executed, dismembered, and his fragmented body scattered conspicuously among Scotland's burgh to discourage his followers. The mob was primed to jeer and stone him every inch of the way. Instead, Montrose's charismatic bearing silenced them or reduced them to tears, while the Marchioness spat from the safety of the balcony, or so the story goes.

William Edmonstone Aytoun's splendidly biased poem relives the scene: 'malignant eyes' watched from the balcony, and the Whig lords' womenfolk were all 'gaunt and withered dames'. Then the confrontation:

> *Then as the Graeme looked upwards,*
> *He saw the ugly smile*
> *Of him who sold his king for gold -*
> *The master-fiend Argyle!*

> *The Marquis gazed a moment,*
> *And nothing did he say,*
> *But the cheek of Argyle grew ghastly pale,*
> *And he turned his eyes away.*

Whatever happened, there is not much chance of winning an objective assessment now, for few people in Scotland's hero-rich history have captured quite so many hearts for quite so long as Montrose. And whatever happened, there is no doubting the verdict of posterity on that singular duel of eyes in the Canongate of May 18, 1650, but for that, we must wait till our own procession reaches St Giles.

It is a short step from the darkest glower of the Canongate around Moray House (where further treacheries were perpetrated, when the signatories of the Treaty of Union fled to a small summer house in the garden to elude the frantic mob and conclude their unsavoury business) to the sweetness and colour-washed light of Chessel's Court. This is another Robert Hurd restoration, one more ray of enlightenment in the architecturally dire days of the 1960s. The courtyard has been completed by new building on its north and east sides, and boasts that rarest of Royal

Chessel's Court: one more ray of enlightenment in the architecturally dire days of the 1960s

Mile landscape features, a lawn. The whole effect is one of an idyllic city centre environment. Idyllic, but for the fact of the re-emergence of the 'no-ball-games-no-children' syndrome which so rules and rankles.

This hounding of ball games actually has a historic precedent hereabouts; it bears all the killjoy hallmarks of the Reformation's persecution of theatre as though it were an anti-social, moral-corrupting evil. Perhaps it was, and perhaps football still is, but how will we ever reinstate the echo of childish laughter to Chessel's Court or mount a serious challenge on the World Cup while our heritage of kicking a tennis ball against a stone wall or making a goal of jackets on a patch of grass is denied?

The Canongate's song is sung, and with it, the first movement of the symphony. To the casual visitor's eye, what follows beyond is simply more of the same street. There is nothing to warn you, but cross that fragment of street which once lay under the shadow of that forbidding and curfewed gateway to Edinburgh, the Netherbow Port, and you step into a quite different world.

The Canongate has never quite got used to the idea that its older burgh status has been usurped, that the city has surrounded it, infiltrated it, almost swamped it. Almost, because there lingers on an instinctive resistance among the natives and those incomers who have been won over by the place and its instincts and its traditions.

The Canongate will never be quite the same place it once was, but neither will its old glories ever fade, or its easy workaday way with its built-in posterity ever wither. From here you can turn and see the sea where its story began. You can turn again and confront that world which beckons up the hill, beyond the ghost of the Netherbow Port - Edinburgh.

T he High Street, Edinburgh, is a world of difference. Almost at once it shakes off the constrictions of the Canongate's deep-shadowed, tight-shackled girth, to become a wider, paler place. Almost at once, too, it becomes a bewilderment of contradictions, in which the last flourish of the twentieth century is trying frantically to rebuild the canyon's breached and fractured walls, while the fifteenth and sixteenth centuries scrutinise its

Royal Mile people: High Street newsvendor; children enthralled at the Museum of Childhood; Mary Croan Bee, whose ancestor established Croan's fish shop in 1883; Ann and John Higgison, Canogotians who 'emigrated' to Hyndford's Close in the High Street in 1987; the Christensen family from Denmark (below right) moved into restored flats at Old Assembly Close in 1989

progress from across the street. The result has a slightly schizophrenic air, the new building too raw and squeaky clean, the old unflatteringly flanked by uninspired neighbours, the street unbridged by a gap five centuries wide, sunlight streaming in through vast holes which should be buildings, and all the stushie and unsettled stoor which chokes the path of transition. It is my best guess, however, that given a quarter of a century of Edinburgh weathering, the 1980s and '90s will survive the old scrutiny passably well. The aberrations of the 1960s and '70s have sunk in, the lessons well learned are being ploughed back into this most fertile field for instinctive architecture. Most important, the new building is falling back on the definitions of the old, which means it is in tune with the symphony.

The first thing you notice, however, is the street itself. It is laid in stone setts where the Canongate is tarmac, and the instant and lasting conclusion of cheek-by-jowl comparison is that stone is right and tarmac is wrong. How on earth was it ever allowed to happen, and how soon can the Canongate win back its old stone carpet?

The second thing you notice is that, amid all the traumas and frustrations of transition, the bottom half of the High Street is no less rich in fascinations - both blatant and bolt-holed - than any other fragment of the Royal Mile. The two oldest houses in Edinburgh and a cluster of vintage closes and a beautifully born-again cinema facade all help to ease the pain of re-birth.

World's End Close is memorable only for its name, for although it dives promisingly gloomy from the street, it ends abruptly in a drab little court. What its name signified, however, was the city's dismissal of what lay beyond, in other words, the Canongate. It should be pointed out that the feeling was mutual - some say it still is - but it was Edinburgh, rather than the Canongate, which took the philosophy to the extreme of nailing it to the wall.

Tweeddale Court, an irresistible lure, reveals the first of its fascinations in an abrupt and daunting barrier, a three-feet-thick stone wall with a pitched crown, perhaps a fragment which harks back to the defensive wall flung round the Edinburgh (but not the Canongate) of 1450. Recent gapsite excavations higher on the High Street unearthed what may well be the

Tweeddale Court

TRUNK'S CLOSE   Richard Demarco

same wall, confirming a line of defence which hugged the street remarkably closely, serving to underline both the city's narrow territorial ambitions and the insecurities of the age. James Grant comments on a contemporary reference to an entreaty with the English after their defeat at the Battle of Sark for a 'renewal of truce'; 'It seemed then to be always 'truce', never peace!' The nature of the Edinburgh and the Royal Mile which we have inherited owes much to that simple foundation-laying truth.

Today, Tweeddale Court inclines towards more peaceable instincts of cultural and literary enterprise. The Scottish Poetry Library is a crucial and long overdue component of old Edinburgh, and there is much on its shelves which found its muse on the street beyond the close-mouth. Fergusson is here, at least! Tweeddale House, home for many generations of the Marquess of Tweeddale's family, and later Oliver and Boyd's old publishing house, is rediscovering its 1576 origins, again as a publishing house. Although Moubray House is across the street, Moubray House Publishing is ensconced here with The List Magazine, established by Robin Hodge who has also been responsible for the thoughtful restoration of the Court. The Saltire Society has moved in next door, abandoning the New Town. This shift, which has its parallels elsewhere in the 1980s revival of the Old Town's spirit, reverses the great rot-inducing defections of earlier eras to the New Town and beyond. Domestic, cultural and commercial life has a stir here again, and social historians of the future will point to our times as one of the Royal Mile's enlightened watersheds.

Tweeddale Court was only memorable until very recently for two of Edinburgh's grizzly murders and the decrepitude of its surroundings (the Royal Mile closes have historic murders like most streets have street lights; an after-dark guided tour can be a singularly thought-provoking experience). For years, the New Palace Cinema was a vile slur on the character of the Royal Mile, but now that its facade has been flatteringly spotlit again - to front new flats - like an ageing, elegant film star's comeback, the word 'PICTURES' gleams out across the street, not in neon but in old carved stone.

Its spade-is-a-spade message appeals, and you occasionally fall to wondering about those modern flats which act out workaday dramas from the one-and-nines! There is nowhere like the Royal Mile for arraying the full repertoire of ingenuity and insult with which one generation can dignify or defile the architecture of its forebears' masterpieces and monstrosities.

South Gray's Close and Hyndford's Close burrow through the newest buildings of the High Street; everything here is vigour and youth, shiny-faced upstarts of buildings with quietly imaginative stone landscaping in the courtyard, but harling and old slate and one venerable rubble wall apiece to act as reference points. The symphony strikes up a jaunty scherzo. John Knox, you feel, would not have approved, but for all the dourness and damnation which history has conferred on his name, his house remains the most charismatic building in the street, the focus of more camera lenses and pointed fingers than perhaps anywhere else in town outside the Castle walls. Its timber galleries are the last survivors of the Royal Mile's sixteenth and seventeenth century hallmark.

Its style is more chaotic than beautiful, and whether Knox ever stayed here is in some doubt, but the association has stuck and although he would have ranted at the very idea, it is what passes for a shrine to the evolution of the religion he preached. It is also - if you conjure a streetful of Knox Houses in your mind's eye - a typical, more-or-less intact, symbol of the High Street Queen Mary would know.

It is also one more modern example of oldest Edinburgh's ability to unmask our ignorance of the unsuspected: a recent restoration un-covered painted panels about which we simply knew nothing. It is right enough that there should be an appropriately conspicuous monument to Knox's ram-stam religion, and its impact on this street, but it would be better for this venerable ancient of Edinburgh's houses to be inhabited, like next door, for example.

Next door is Moubray House, like John Knox House, a sixteenth and seventeenth century development of fifteenth century origins. That the place should have a presence is hardly surprising. Nothing can survive 500 years without absorbing and emitting intangibles. What accords it a kind of magic is the sense of that intangible which derives from contin-uous habitation. Its top floor eyrie is warmly lived in under a half-barrel vaulted ceiling, and on floors and stairs with a gradient characteristic of much of the street itself.

The High Street in close-up including a relic of the demolished Netherbow Port, the top-floor kitchen of Moubray House and embellishments to John Knox's House Far right: Knox's House, symbol of the High Street Mary, Queen of Scots, would know

GOD · ABVFE · AL · AND · YI · NYC

PICTURES

DEOS DEVS GOD

NETHERBOW

13

Chalmers Close   Richard DeMarco

Chalmers Close is an unpromising diversion, and the invitation to visit the new Brass Rubbing Centre gives little indication of the barely credible story of Trinity College Church Hall which lies concealed halfway down. It is a grim enough journey; the foot of the close baulks at a stupefying concrete-and-glass office building, but just when you are convinced the close has no saving grace, you encounter the most baffling church building you have ever seen. What on earth is it?

It is this: Trinity College Church, much lamented as one of Scotland's best mediaeval buildings, had the misfortune to have been built (in the fifteenth century) in the path of the head of steam generated by the Victorian enthusiasm for railways. Incredibly, it was demolished, the stones numbered and stacked to await the day when it would be rebuilt. Nothing in Edinburgh, before or since the arrival of the railway, musters quite the speed of execution which the urgency of the situation demands, however. By the time the rebuilding-by-numbers was put in hand, so many of its stones had been spirited away that there was just enough for this sad, faint echo of older glories.

Lord Cockburn, Edinburgh's eloquent conservation pioneer remarked memorably: *These people would remove Pompeii for a railway and tell us they had applied it to better use in Dundee.* Geddes condemned it thus: *This railway system . . . has been not merely half ruinous to the beauty of Edinburgh, but structurally bungled and economically wasteful to all concerned.*

The bungling, the ruinousness, the wastefulness, celebrated arguably their finest hour here. To see just how grotesque is the sorry fate of what is left of Trinity College Church, clamber up the back outside stair of Bailie Fyfe's Close and look back, and bear in mind as you look back that 500 years ago, it was majestic. There is nothing wrong with a brass rubbing centre, and certainly the new sign on the building makes a passable attempt at dignifying the place, but there are many people, even today, who have never forgiven the railway's brass neck.

Bailie Fyfe's Close has a more memorable claim to fame than a bird's-eye-view of a deformed relic, however. It was here in 1863 that a 250-year-old tenement suddenly gave up its old stone ghost, and simply sank to the ground, killing 35 people. The frantic search for bodies in the

rubble was accorded an immortality from the lips of a boy who was trapped. He shouted, 'Heave awa' chaps, I'm no dead yet!' and in that instant gave Edinburgh's vocabulary an all-purpose response to troublesome circumstances. The boy is commemorated above the mouth of nearby Paisley Close, but his spirit and his evocative cry have won wider memorials.

The Royal Mile has now climbed to that point in its story - the junction with the North and South Bridges - after which nothing was ever the same again. The North Bridge would lead the defection away from the Old Town; the South Bridge would sprawl the city away to the Pentlands; the east-west canyon was irreparably breached. Three of the four corner buildings of that uneasy junction are of those other worlds, other eras. One of the three was recently converted to flats and marketed as 'Royal Mile Mansions' but has as much to do with the Royal Mile or its true mansions as a rubble wall on a Georgian Terrace.

Ah, but the fourth corner building is easy to fall in love with! It is the Tron Kirk which has survived all manner of discomforts and disfigurements and won through with a robust and warm vigour. It is a place with a stone-built personality, and when, in 1987, the fledgling Edinburgh Old Town Trust set about its rot-stopping, stoor-stirring work, it seized on the Tron as its symbol.

At this point, the church had been closed for 35 years, stripped of its furnishing, and had nothing with which to sell itself other than its own personality, and the intriguing 1970s excavations of the mediaeval alley of Marlin's Wynd, which had simply been buried in the Tron's foundations. The Trust wanted the Tron reopened, as a declaration of intent, and in an absurdly short space of time achieved just that, convinced that enough people would find the simple exhibition and the story of the building and the excavation enough of a lure. With no advertising and no admission charge, 33,000 people found their way in to its charmed embrace in five months.

The reopening of the Tron also provided another service, which was to effect - however fleetingly and inadequately - a small celebration of

The Tron Kirk: *has survived all manner of discomforts and disfigurements and won through with a robust and warm vigour*

Overpage: the Royal Mile in high summer; kitsch and culture

Robert Fergusson. His birthplace in Cap and Feather Close was obliterated in the building of the North Bridge, but it is clear from his poem *To the Tron-Kirk Bell* that he was over-familiar with sight and sound of the Tron for his own liking. The re-opened Kirk narrated it:

> *Wanwordy, crazy, dinsome thing,*
> *As e'er was fram'd to jow or ring,*
> *What gar'd them sic in steeple hing*
> *They ken themsel',*
> *But well wat I they couldna bring*
> *War sounds frae hell.*

There is much more exquisite vitriol. What marks Fergusson out for fitter tribute than he has won thus far from his city is his ability to draw vividly on this street and its closes and characters and conventions. His is an art which sprung from the very stones themselves, and that fact and his unarguable effect on Burns makes enough of a case for a lasting memorial. As the city ponders at its own characteristic pace, a lasting solution to the problem of what to do with the Tron Kirk, they could do worse than consider Robert Fergusson, Poet, for its theme:

> *If magistrates wi' me wud 'gree,*
> *For ay tongue-tackit shud you be,*
> *Nor fleg wi' antimelody*
> *Sic honest folk,*
> *Whase lugs were never made to dree*
> *Thy doolfu' shock.*

Fergusson eventually had his way. The Tron Bell has long been tongue-tackit, its congregation likewise, but bell and god-fearing folk still raise their anthems up-bye at St Giles, the High Kirk, one-time Cathedral, and long-time landmark.

The Royal Mile has suffered from delusions of grandeur in the precincts of St Giles for 350 years. Even today, it affords itself unaccustomed light and breadth, where once it sat ominously hemmed in. Tenements once

The High Kirk of
St Giles: *a brave bulk*
throwing vast shadows
across the street

61

clambered the walls of St Giles like regimented ivy, and the thrumming of the luckenbooth traders, and the daily ritual of merchants and businessmen gathering at the Mercat Cross, made a merry chaos.

It was George Drummond during one of his Lord Provostships who sought to dignify the process with a Royal Exchange, and suiting the action to the notion, had it built, the way he seemed to be able to do. It was beautifully built, too, round a discreet square marked by a noble arcade. Drummond failed, however, to break the habits of thousands of lifetimes, and business burgeoned as before in all Edinburgh's weathers while, for once, Drummond's dream withered and the empty exchange echoed his sighs. Edinburgh Corporation, later Edinburgh District Council, has long since adopted it as the City Chambers, so at least Drummond passed his planned dignity on to his descendants in the highest civic office. The ordered courtyard, to John Adam's design of 1753, conceals behind its back an eleven-storey plunge to Cockburn Street. The demands of nature as architect have never relented.

But if Drummond's Old Town memorial is not all he might have wished for it, the fate which befell Parliament House on the far side of St Giles gave rise to a sickness which Scotland has never shaken off. This was to be the building which brought the Parliament of Scotland down out of the Castle and into the midst of its people. It survived as that Parliament from 1639 until 1707, when it performed its ultimate disservice and flitted to Westminster. It is small wonder that the mob hounded the signatories to all manner of unparliamentary bolt-holes.

Parliament House is still a fine building - on the inside at least, where a stupendous ceiling survives - although nineteenth century external resurfacing has done it no favours, and introduced a blatant discord into the old symphony. Lord Cockburn ranted at the transformation, and anyone peering down from George IV Bridge at the one surviving wall of the original can see how right he was to rant. The place is no longer Parliament House, of course, but merely Parliament Hall, an adjunct to the courts of law, and the sole preserve of the legal profession.

It is not without a certain impressive bustle, but the descendants of the mob see here only a limp symbol of what Edinburgh has become, a capital city of a nation denied nationhood. It was always

St Giles stained glass: the modern Robert Burns memorial (left) contrasts sharply with more traditional windows

arguable that Scotland's nationhood could have survived well enough under a dual monarchy with England, but it was in this street, and the abandoning of this building, that a heartbeat stopped. No amount of developed compromise has massaged it back to life, not in 280 years.

The High Kirk of St Giles is a brave bulk throwing vast winter shadows across the street, according Edinburgh's world famous old skyline its most distinguished embellishment. The restoration appeal fund says it has been at the heart of city and nation for more than a thousand years. If it is a justifiable claim, it is less true today than it ever was. Somehow its many restorations and rebuilds and re-thinks have conspired to disrobe it of its spirituality, so that it seems a darkly unemotional Kirk within.

The earliest remnants, always such a potently articulate voice elsewhere in the Royal Mile, look somehow drowned out by the clamour of later alterations. Curiously, it is the twentieth century which, of all its later eras, has served St Giles best. The Thistle Chapel of 1909-1911 is poignant and perfect, the gift of the 12th Earl of Leven and his brothers, their worthy compromise to their father's futile deathbed wish to restore Holyrood's ancient ruin. Here there is intimacy, grace, a spiritual awe which the body of the High Kirk conspicuously lacks. Here too, amid much exquisite craftsmanship, an angel plays the bagpipes, and there are few enough pipers in Edinburgh who play like angels.

The twentieth century has also given St Giles the West Window, a 1985 memorial to Robert Burns, 'poet of humanity', by an Icelandic artist, Leifur Breidfjord. Like much of what has gone before in the High Kirk, it was the subject of high controversy. I love it, for it strikes at least one optimistic note within, a thing of vigour and colour, a new bravery to match the old one aloft on the skyline. In a barely visible memorial, Robert Louis Stevenson is remembered here too.

Perhaps when the restoration work is complete, and St Giles re-emerges from its self-inflicted gloom, we can feel at ease there again. It would be good to be able to; any edifice which has been at the heart of the nation for a thousand years should evoke an instant instinctive response in the natives. But, like the stilled pulse of Parliament House, there is a heart here too which wearies for the want of coursing lifeblood.

At the heart of the nation for a thousand years: Sir Walter Scott contemplates St Giles from Princes Street

There was, you may remember, to be a reckoning in St Giles of that fateful day in 1650, when the doomed Montrose and the partying Argyll set hateful eyes on each other, and it is this: Charles II had Montrose's remains reassembled and laid to rest here, and his effigy lies spotlit and never without flowers. Eleven years after his death, Argyll his betrayer, was also executed, and (so legend at least avows) Montrose's head was removed from a spike on the nearby Tolbooth, to make way for Argyll's. Argyll lies now by the far wall across the Kirk of St Giles, darkened and unremembered. They are queer bedfellows but who knows what dark exchanges cross the Kirk on a pale May night?

It is a salutory commentary, whatever, on the ways of history's bloody fervours and fads and the flimsy and fleeting frailties of those who champion their God. St Giles, whatever its temporary failings, has played host to a wheen of ghosts within its many walls.

We had always known that Marlin's Wynd - and Mary King's Close under the City Chambers - were there to be rediscovered in some shape or form, but in Advocate's Close in 1985, there emerged another of those time-warping old stone ghosts which took everyone by surprise. Edinburgh's story is so old, so worn, so scrutinised, so analysed, so devoured, so divulged, so told and retold and written and re-written, that if it were almost anywhere else, an unsuspected chapter would be preposterous. But we have long since learned the capacity of the Royal Mile to hoard and hide itself away from the gaze of centuries. Now in its fractured ribcage, the signature of a fifteenth century stonemason emerged from its chrysalis of centuries. The signature, a scratching of crosses, is his last small flourish on a fireplace of regal proportions, which was incarcerated in seventeenth century panelling and thrust by some stone-contemptuous interior designer into a cramped corner of would-be oblivion.

Alas for oblivion, Advocate's Close stumbled into the hands of the planning department of Edinburgh District Council and came under the thoughtful scrutiny of the Old Town Committee for Conservation and Renewal (kindred spirits to the Edinburgh Old Town Trust in the re-awakening of the Old Town) during their search for an appropriate permanent home. Such providential flukes are thin on the ground, but

Anchor Close

Assembly Close

Richard Demarco

one of the principals of the reawakening process has been Ian Begg, architect, Royal Mile resident, romantic, idealist, and crucially, disciple and, for many years, partner of Robert Hurd.

A day or two after the discovery, I followed Ian Begg up a perilous clutter of makeshift props and steel pipes to play my journalist's instincts on the anonymous craftsman and his 500-year-old art. The room was tiny, lit only by a hastily slung light bulb, and the constant building site barrow-bustle of bricks and mortar and banter could easily have stifled any sense of wonder. But Ian Begg is not easily deflected from his infectious enthusiasms, and as he speculated about the whys and where-fores of a fireplace of royal palace proportions in a room the size of a generous cupboard, it was clear even in that gloom, that he had unearthed a new Royal Mile mystery. It is the joy of this street that such things can happen.

I see that stonemason tap out his own immortality at the hearth of a great hall in which he laboured for - for how many years of his life? I see him shoulder his tools and file with his fellows out into the evening of his stone city, its teeming single street and its stench. I see him go. I mourn his passing. The descent down out of such a room is inevitably an anti-climax, a train of thought derailed by more barrowloads of the twentieth century's rebuilding ways, but even as you dust down your clothes, you fall to wondering just how old some of that dust might be.

Two more fireplaces have since emerged, a fragment of wall-hung fabric, hints of very old wall paintings. The Committee and the Trust are now in residence here, the fireplaces standing proud in offices for which they were never designed, but offices whose occupants are dedicated to the wellbeing of the stonemason's descendants and the heritage he helped to build. There is a kind of chaotic logic at work which it is better not to question.

Another breach in the canyon wall heralds the end of another move-ment of the symphony, throws a bridge south over the perceptibly steepening valley, plunges down the Mound into the old Nor' Loch valley. From here on, the Royal Mile becomes first the

Royal Mile embellishments, fragments and memorials

Lawnmarket then Castlehill, climbing and narrowing into an aggressive defence of the Castle itself, which now peers down through the roof-ragged street.

This crossroads is a good place from which to observe the character of the street (and the middle of the junction, is the best). There is a far sea glitter and a blaze of green marking Holyrood and beyond, where everything began; and there is the first conspicuous suggestion of castellated might where the beginning had its end. Look back down the wake of your progress. You mark the street's sudden dip from sight below the Tron Kirk, with only the walls of the canyon marking its riverbed's path.

The Canongate is unguessable from here, lost in its other world; there is the High Street and Holyrood and the sea and this rock-solid heartbeat of Edinburgh reassuring your stance. There are special times for imbibing the intricacies of the street's distance, offering not just sights but insights. The best of these is the hush hour, an Edinburgh phenomenon, a profound calm which settles like benevolent snow in the early evening. The workaday capital city din has subsided, and before the lesser bustle of the night, the place slows and stills.

In late spring or early summer, the evening sun is still high enough to throw a mellow, tawny ambience down the hill and strike colour and shadow and emphasis on unsuspected eminences and blatant pre-eminences. St Giles blackens, the Tron pales, John Knox House's pantiles are embers, the canyon walls soften for an hour to an almost pliable grace. The symphony is at its most seductive. Conduct it from the podium of the Gladstone's Land steps, where the glittering kite and its prey instil wilder bewitchments. Like all good seductions, it is over too soon. The sun dowses, the light flattens, the stone hardens, grays, the city stirs and the thing is gone. To have seen it, though, is to have seen the aurora borealis, set in stone.

For all the street-poetry, life's hidden prose lurks all around. The north side of the Lawnmarket is the best of the Royal Mile's courtyards, a spacious string of them, punctuated by houses of old distinctions like Lady Stair's House with its bold hexagonal stair tower. It would be better lived in again, however, than reduced to its uninspired status of literary museum (locks of hair, Walter Scott's knife and fork, that kind of thing)

Gladstone's Land:
where the glittering kite and its prey instil wilder bewitchments

71

*Gladstone's Land is a
museum to the life of
the street itself, a
condemned slum when
it came into the hands
of the National Trust
for Scotland*

Mylne's Court

Richard Demarco

Lawnmarket: *a sure
sense of place and
timelessness*

to Scott and Burns and Stevenson. No Fergusson for all it was his street not theirs.

Gladstone's Land is also a museum, but a museum to the life of the street itself. A narrow six-storey tenement built in 1617-20, a supreme testimony to the worth of the National Trust for Scotland. It was a condemned slum - like much of the Old Town - when it came into the Trust's hands in 1934. Now painted ceiling and walls, the original street front onto which Thomas Gledstanes had grafted a new and internally elegant frontage, a green room ('well hidden under 14 layers of paint') have all re-emerged, and the house has been re-equipped with contemporary furnishings. Its story, and the story of the Royal Mile merchant who gave it its name are fundamentals of the Royal Mile's living history. This house is an object lesson in the telling of such stories.

The courts lead on through James Court with its three entries, to the model for all the Royal Mile's courtyards, Mylne's Court of 1690. It commemorates its architect Robert Mylne, who as His Majesty's Master Mason was a signatory to the royal contract to rebuild Holyrood Palace in 1672. It is no meagre immortality which the Royal Mile accords him.

The south side of the Lawnmarket is unendowed with these spacious high-flanked courtyards (although there is a wonderfully quirky outside first floor timber staired secret stashed away in Brodie's Close, and Riddles Court has a double surprise) but its street front is as impressive as anything anywhere, and from down the Mile a bit, the effect of the perspective on a street which narrows as it climbs, is one of a well-thought stone collage. The rubble and the ashlar cheek-by-jowl it here to great effect, and for all the razzmatazz and tartanry which dominates the ground floor, it is in the Lawnmarket that you win back that sure sense of place and timelessness which stamped itself on your first glimpse up the Canongate from the Abbey Strand.

Castlehill beckons with an almost dour defiance of your acceptance. The Tolbooth Highland St John Kirk, which has sold its ecclesiastical soul to the mammon of the heritage business, albeit to one of the best in that business, is a daunting sentinel as the canyon narrows and dwindles up its last measured steps to the Castle. What steps have clambered here over the years with quickening pulse? It is a dark, almost

Ramsay Garden:
outrageous, romantic,
inspsired, the stroke of
a very daring genius

drab place, well endowed only in tourist trappings and unexceptional buildings, until with its last gesture it presents, first Canonball House, with its innumerable crowstep gables, and an intriguing throwback to the mediaeval custom of wooden shutters which slip over the windows on stone runners; then, wonder of wonders, Ramsay Garden.

If you come to the Royal Mile fresh and unsuspecting, Ramsay Garden is an astonishment, like, say, two White Horse Closes stuck one on top of the other with added embellishments and the whole transported to a small mountain top. It is the one place in the entire street which can lay claim to beauty. It is outrageous, romantic, inspired, the stroke of a very daring genius. It was Patrick Geddes at work, practising what he preached about the re-birth of the Royal Mile by trying to lure university professors, convinced in the reforming zeal which would be its ultimate spin-off. He saw even in the wretched decay of the place in the late nineteenth century how it might blossom again, and seized on the house of Alan Ramsay the poet as the cornerstone of his creation.

He created much more of course, because he would inspire many others like Robert Hurd, and so set in motion a chain reaction of inspiration which galvanises still. The Royal Mile has been a progressively better place since the day he first turned his eye on it and acknowledged that it was a street with a future as well as a quite matchless past. He may not have composed the symphony in old stone, but he (more than most of recent times) orchestrated it with on a human scale with taste and authority and a sure ear for its rhythms and songs.

T he Esplanade of Edinburgh Castle should be crossed swiftly. It is an unkempt, run-down, patched and cracked tarmac prairie, flanked by an ad-hoc guddle of unimpressive and unexceptional memorials. Its only saving grace is the sudden sprawled girth of the Castle itself, and sightlines to every horizon bar the west: to Pentland Hills, city and sea, the Forth and Fife. An opportunity to transform it into a bold and skillful permanent arena was offered in a Government-commissioned feasibility study by architect Geoffrey Jarvis in 1986, but after two years of deliberation, the Scottish Office declined the challenge and opted for £6 million

The Esplanade: *an ad-hoc guddle of unimpressive and unexceptional memorials' including Earl Haig and his horse, shuttered from tourist season eyes by the Tattoo stands*

worth of internal improvements. If we accept that Edinburgh Castle's role today is primarily one of symbolism and heritage (and privileged familiarity for those who live and work every day in its shadow), then our own era has lost an opportunity of rare significance.

Beyond, and within, through the six gates, however, Edinburgh Castle still has many powers to captivate and to confirm the instinct of those first settlers who eyed the rock from the sea and uttered the word 'fortify' in their own tongue. Its size inside, particularly its height, always catches me out, and the hands of the stonemasons of almost every century since the twelfth are detectable to one extent or another. The true age of its origins are still only guessable, but who will be surprised if excavations begun in 1988 uncover the spoor of a millenium more?

The Castle is a book in itself, a series of books, a small library of books if you detail the lives of those who have strutted its stage and forged and fouled their destinies here. It remains a place of awesome power, evokes bewilderment of responses, a Mons Meg of a castle. An information board in the vaults articulates its significance in the sixteenth century thus: *The Castle then stood at the summit of its preeminence: fortress, palace, arsenal, treasury, state prison and repository of the national archives: it was the chief place of ceremony in the kingdom where great banquets and state assemblies, including Parliament, were held.* From primitive speculative fortress to the all-purpose hub of a nation . . . it is a singular progress and a singular story. Today its buildings range from the languishing sunless vaults to the tiny, simple, sacred and endearing chamber of St Margaret's Chapel, to Sir Robert Lorimer's overwhelming Scottish National War Museum for the First World War. Its military archive is stupendous, its history matchless, its presence matched - some say out-matched - only by Stirling Castle, 40 miles upriver.

Its essence for me distils, however clumsily and inadequately, into a threefold symbolic response.

The first is to confront and marvel at Mons Meg, the cannon. To throw her adjectives like 'great' or 'mighty' is to belittle the beast. To have her on your side in her heyday was to win. Her? A piece of artillery with a personality? You must go and stand and stare and judge for yourself. Cromwell did not doubt it, for one. His inventory of captured guns lists

The Castle: *from primitive speculative fortress to the all-purpose hub of a nation*

NEMO·ME·IMPUNE·LACESSIT

'the great iron murderer, Meg'. Sir Walter Scott rescued her from ignominity in the Tower of London, and brought her home with an escort, from Leith, of three troops of cavalry and a pipe band. How often has such tribute been accorded to an obsolete gun? She thrives now in her role as superstar in retirement, the more tourist bustle about her the more blatant her contemptuous aloofness. She did it all. She exerts the kind of influence hereabouts that Mary has won in Holyrood, heroines both who lived in daring times and were not found wanting. She fired a salute for Mary's first wedding. The missile travelled two miles.

My second response is altogether more solemn, more private, more idealistic, more romantic, more nationalistic. It is to ponder might-have-beens in the gilded and pearled company of the Scottish regalia. The Crown Room is a place to come upon in one of the Castle's quieter hours, because it symbolises that which is lost, which all Scots - and many non-Scots - hold deep and dear. Some will qualify the degree to which they will own up to the sentiment of loss, but none can deny the instinct.

The sword's traverse ends in two acorns, unplanted seeds of who knows what manner of mighty oaks? I am not the first to be moved by the encased symbolism of the Scottish regalia. It was Scott again whose steadfast patriotism won them back for their home and their people. Like much else which was subdued by the Union, the regalia suffered the persecution of concealment, on the basis that out of sight was out of the minds of the disapproving mob. George IV finally responded to Sir Walter's campaign in 1817 and ordered the long-locked Crown Room (closed for twenty-three years) to be opened, to ascertain whether the regalia still existed, or whether, as many by then had begun to believe, they had been removed to England.

It was a sweet, sweet, moment for Sir Walter Scott and Scotland. To have been there must have been to dwell briefly on a higher plane than most of us achieve. Sir Walter wrote it: *It was with feelings of no common anxiety that the commissioners having read their warrant, proceeded to the crown-room, and having found all there in the state in which it had been left in 1794, the last time the room had been opened, during a search for lost Parliamentary records, commanded the king's smith, who was in attendance, to force open the great chest, the keys of which had been sought*

A Mons Meg of a Castle

for in vain. The general impression that the regalia had been secretly removed weighed heavily on the hearts of all while the labour proceeded. The chest seemed to return a hollow and empty sound to the strokes of the hammer; and even those whose expectations had been most sanguine felt at that moment the probability of bitter disappointment, and could not but be sensible that, should the result of the search confirm those forebodings, it would only serve to show that a national affront - an injury had been sustained, for which it might be difficult, or rather impossible, to obtain redress. The joy was therefore extreme when, the ponderous lid of the chest having been forced open, at the expense of some time and labour, the regalia were discovered lying at the bottom covered with linen cloths, exactly as they had been left in 1707, being 110 years before, since they had been surrendered by William the ninth Earl Marischal to the custody of the Earl of Glasgow, Treasurer-Deputy of Scotland. The reliques were passed from hand to hand, and greeted with the affectionate reverence which emblems so venerable, restored to public view after a slumber of more than a hundred years, were so peculiarly calculated to excite. The discovery was instantly communicated to the public by the display of the Royal Standard, and was greeted by the shouts of the soldiers in the garrison and a vast multitude assembled on the Castle Hill; indeed the rejoicing was so general and sincere as plainly to show that, however altered in other respects, the people of Scotland had lost nothing of that national enthusiasm which formerly had displayed itself in grief for the loss of those emblematic honours, and now was expressed in joy for their recovery.

My third distillation of the essence of Edinburgh Castle is to make the small pilgrimage to St Margaret's Chapel. Many people who come to the Royal Mile today will prefer to walk down it rather than climb it, because it is easier. It denies, however, the perspective which falls into place with the attainment of this rough and ready wind-washed end. Within, it is a subtle place, white and subtle and simple - pure, I think - set with small, vivid stained glass windows, and the perpetual flowers which uphold a good tradition. It is that each week, a woman called Margaret, a member of the St Margaret's Chapel Guild, puts flowers in the chapel.

It is as simple and appropriate as that. It is a commemoration of a quite

The Castle's military archive is stupendous, its history matchless

ST. MARGARET'S CHAPEL.

MARGARET

From here
you watched, enshrined,
and wept

while Wallace
Bruce and Stuarts and all
their weary warlords

rose and fell
to the tunes
of dire destinies.

You crown all
Scotland's crowns, not goldly,
not gloriously,

but with one
small and still
white room -

guardhouse of truth,
prison of patience,
chamber of remembrance

which endures
its own eternity. Only
the first millenium

is almost over,
Margaret.

remarkable familiarity, as though she had died a year ago, rather than 900 years. Ronald Selby Wright writes in the Chapel booklet: . . . will you come in imagination out of the world into a few minutes of God's peace, and go back again to whatever work you have to do, renewed and re-freshed, feeling that it was good to have been there. The booklet's 21st reprint in 1984 denoted 1,250,000 copies since the first printing in 1957. Queen Margaret, the saint, wins hearts and minds still, and it does not matter what manner of God you hold to . . . it will have been good to be here.

I wrote the first draft of much of this book on a string of warm, early spring days in a replica mediaeval garden off the Canongate. It is, like so many adjuncts to the Royal Mile, a quiet place. It lies snug in that 'little valley between two mountains' once overrun by the forest of Drumsheugh and its king-hunting stags. It feels as irrelevant to the small solaces of St Margaret's Chapel as the old Canongate must once have felt to Edinburgh. One is ancient, and one is quite new. Yet they are both weavings of the same thread, the thread spun by the first land-wary seamen who dared the rock in its wilderness.

It is the thread which matters now, for the Royal Mile is in the throes of one of its many eras of transition. Some will ask with some justification, when was it not in transition, and why therefore whould we treat it differently now? The answer is that now we know the worth of heritage. We have learned not to obliterate and rebuild second best when restoration is preferable (and we have learned to restore better than any of our ancestors). We have known since Geddes, perhaps since Lord Cockburn, that there is merit in the spirit of the mediaeval town for its own sake. It matters because it has been.

We have also begun to learn - more recently - that there is no merit in perpetuating the spirit if the Royal Mile which evolves by our guidance is not populated by our own kind. The population has begun to rise again, by the deliberate application of enlightened policy. That in turn has heightened the popular esteem in which the street is held. It all strengthens the thread.

The standards of what, and how, and where we rebuild and

*now we know the worth
of heritage*

restore are high; we must be sure they are high enough. Second best or worse is inadequate for the street. It is inadequate not because of some ill-judged egotistical assessment of our own capital city importance, but because we must do justice to the legacy which is ours, both in terms of built stone and our own instinctive sense of what is right for the Royal Mile. Do we always use architects and developers who are at ease and at one with that instinct, and dare we ever do otherwise, now that we know so much of what has been and the fragmentary worth of what remains? Our standards strengthen the thread.

We have also to resolve the dilemmas of tourism which are the price and the privilege we pay for our heritage; it is not always convenient to have the world beat a path to our doorstep, but it is a magnificent accolade. Dangers lie in pandering to the accolade at the expense of the local population.

The Scottish Tourist Board sees in the Royal Mile untapped potential, potential to swell tourism's coffers, to flatter tourism's statistics, to enrich the experience of visitors, to sell the city and the nation to the world, and they are right. Meanwhile the lured-back population bemoans the absence of a butcher, a grocer, a reliable car parking space, and they are right. We don't demolish old unworshipped churches any more, but we are more likely to convert them into visitor entertainments rather than enhancing the quality of life of the congregation of the street. So striking the balance and being fearfully aware of permitting imbalances will strengthen the thread.

The portents are optimistic. The street is in good heart. Not only is the world recognising the fact, but Edinburgh is recognising it too. There is a creative stir about the Royal Mile, and that will strengthen the thread.

The thread is the lifeblood of the street, the teller of its story, the champion of its people, the rhythm of the symphony. It was woven in many conflicts. Who is to say now that it will not weave again of its best, now that the truce has granted the peace?

ROYAL MILE

All Scotland's skyline
assembles in that sharp frieze
of stalagmites
spired and spiky
as thistles
rooted in the sediments
of ice age architecture.

Dynasties and definitions
of Gods and kings and architects
lie layered beneath
the street's consuming dust.
Each time it rains
it gardyloos
some era-encrusted reformist blood
or other clean away.

A kirk astride a close
(a crushed townhouse
for a crypt)
is nothing new. To walk
an hour amid
such stony company
is to hear retold
to see unfold the story
and the exquisite agony
which is Scotland.

*Nature is
the chief architect of
the Old Town of
Edinburgh. A volcanic
plug and its glacial tail
offered a defendable
plinth*

I wrote the first draft of much of this book on a string of warm, early spring days in a replica mediaeval garden off the Canongate. It is, like so many adjuncts to the Royal Mile, a quiet place. It lies snug in that 'little valley between two mountains' once overrun by the forest of Drumsheugh and its king-hunting stags. It feels as irrelevant to the small solaces of St Margaret's Chapel as the old Canongate must once have felt to Edinburgh. One is ancient, and one is quite new. Yet they are both weavings of the same thread, the thread spun by the first land-wary seamen who dared the rock in its wilderness